EVERYDAY
WISDOM

More Books by Dr. Wayne W. Dyer

<u>BOOKS</u>

Counseling Effectively in Groups
Counseling Techniques That Work
Getting in the Gap (book-with-CD)
Gifts from Eykis
Group Counseling for Personal Mastery
Manifest Your Destiny
No More Holiday Blues
The Power of Intention
A Promise Is a Promise
Pulling Your Own Strings
Real Magic
The Sky's the Limit
Staying on the Path
10 Secrets for Success and Inner Peace
There Is a Spiritual Solution to Every Problem
What Do You Really Want for Your Children?
Wisdom of the Ages
You'll See It When You Believe It
Your Erroneous Zones
Your Sacred Self

Please visit Hay House USA: www.hayhouse.com; Hay House Australia:
www.hayhouse.com.au; Hay House UK: www.hayhouse.co.uk;
Hay House South Africa: orders@psdprom.co.za

EVERYDAY
WISDOM

Dr. Wayne W. Dyer

HAY HOUSE, INC.
Carlsbad, California
London • Sydney • Johannesburg
Vancouver • Hong Kong

Published and distributed in the United States by: Hay House, Inc., P.O. Box 5100, Carlsbad, CA 92018-5100 • *Phone:* (760) 431-7695 or (800) 654-5126 • *Fax:* (760) 431-6948 or (800) 650-5115 • www.hayhouse.com • *Published and distributed in Australia by:* Hay House Australia Pty. Ltd., 18/36 Ralph St., Alexandria NSW 2015 • *Phone:* 612-9669-4299 • *Fax:* 612-9669-4144 • www.hayhouse.com.au • *Published and distributed in the United Kingdom by:* Hay House UK, Ltd. • Unit 62, Canalot Studios • 222 Kensal Rd., London W10 5BN • *Phone:* 44-20-8962-1230 • *Fax:* 44-20-8962-1239 • www.hayhouse.co.uk • *Published and distributed in the Republic of South Africa by:* Hay House SA (Pty), Ltd., P.O. Box 990, Witkoppen 2068 • *Phone/Fax:* 2711-7012233 • orders@psdprom.co.za • *Distributed in Canada by:* Raincoast • 9050 Shaughnessy St., Vancouver, B.C. V6P 6E5 • *Phone:* (604) 323-7100 • *Fax:* (604) 323-2600

Editorial supervision: Jill Kramer   *Design:* Amy Gingery

The material in this book is from *Everyday Wisdom* by Wayne Dyer, © 1993, Hay House, Inc.

Library of Congress Control Number: 2004101504

ISBN 1-4019-0505-6

08 07 06 05 4 3 2 1
1st printing, February 2005

Printed in Canada

To Barbara Bergen
with appreciation and love

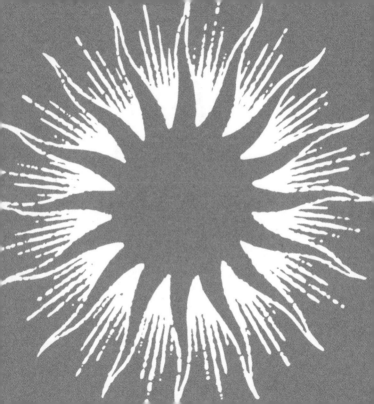

"I've learned many things from my friend, guide, and mentor, Dr. Wayne Dyer. Even a single phrase from his books and speeches can help transform your life. *Everyday Wisdom* has many guides that will serve you on your path to transformation."
— **Deepak Chopra, M.D.**

"Wayne Dyer has always reflected the power of inner guidance in his work. In *Everyday Wisdom,* he gives you the gems of his *own* inner wisdom and helps you recognize the wonderful miracles that you have within yourself."
— **Louise L. Hay**

You're not a human being having a

spiritual experience. You're a spiritual

being having a human experience.

All the abundance
you want is already here.
You just have to tune it in.

Three things clog
your soul: negativity,
judgment, and imbalance.

Everything in the universe flows.

You can't get ahold of water by

clutching it. Let your hand relax,

though, and then you can experience it.

The whole universal system is held

together through love, harmony, and

cooperation. If you use your thoughts

according to these principles, you can

transcend anything that gets in your way.

Perhaps you'll be surprised
to learn that there's no such
thing as a nervous breakdown.
Nerves don't break down.
People choose to.

Having a plan isn't necessarily

unhealthy, but falling in love

with the plan is a real neurosis . . .

don't let your plan

become bigger than you are.

Thoughts, when properly nourished and internalized, will become a reality in your world of form. Thoughts are extremely powerful things.

Ultimately, there's nothing to forgive, because there's nothing to judge and no one to blame.

Positive thoughts

keep you in harmony

with the universe.

Traffic, in and of itself,

can never irritate anybody.

It just does what it does.

Traffic doesn't care!

We can only give away
to others what we have
inside ourselves.

Be willing to let

anything happen.

Each time you send love
in response to hate,
you diffuse the hate.

Forgiveness is
an act of
self-love.

If you step back

far enough, it's easy to see

humanity as one.

What you see
is evidence of what
you believe.
Believe it and you'll see it.

All your behavior

results from the thoughts

that precede it.

In reality, it's much easier
not to smoke or eat chocolate
than to do so. It's your mind
that convinces you otherwise.

Anything you must have

comes to own you.

Ironically, when you release it,

you start getting more of it.

In order to make a visualization a reality in the world of form, you must be willing to do whatever it takes to make it happen.

Whatever the question,

love is the answer.

I once gave the refrigerator repairman
several of my books and tapes. The
repairman asked, "How do you ever
expect to make any money when you
give away all your stuff?" I replied,
"When the day comes that you don't
have to ask me that question,
you'll have the answer."

Nothing is formed.
Nothing dies. Everything is
simply in transition.

If you control your thoughts,

and your feelings come from your

thoughts, then you control

your feelings.

If you only believe
what you see, then you're
limited to what's on the
surface. If you only believe
what you see, why do you
pay your electric bill?

If you're going to change
a habit, you must *be*
the treatment.

No one can create anger

or stress within you.

Only you can do that

by virtue of how

you process your world.

29

"No-limit people" don't say,
"I'm going to get it all."
They say, "I am it all already,
but I can grow."

No one knows enough

to be a pessimist.

No amount of guilt

can ever change history.

No amount of guilt

can ever change anything.

Blame is a neat little device that you can use whenever you don't want to take responsibility for something in your life. Use it and you'll avoid all risks and impede your own growth.

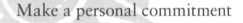

Make a personal commitment

to do what you love and

love what you do—today!

Be the cure.
Don't look
outside yourself
for it.

If prayer is you talking

to God, then intuition is

God talking to you.

Listen to those inner signals
that help you make
the right choices—no matter
what anyone thinks.

37

Trust your
intuitive voices
and go with them.

Learn to find the blessing in pain.

Practice observing the pain

rather than owning it.

Loving sacredly means loving

what is, even if you don't comprehend

the deeper meaning behind it.

Behavior is a much better barometer of what you are than words.

I'm grateful to all
those people who said no.
It's because of them
that I did it all myself.

Every obstacle

is an opportunity.

Every obstacle is a test.

Emotions are choices.

Doing what you love

is the cornerstone of having

abundance in your life.

Deficiency-motivated people

spend their lives in the disease

called *more*—always trying to acquire

something to make themselves feel

complete and to repair the deficiency.

Conflict is a violation of harmony. If you participate in it, you're part of the problem, not the solution.

Don't let emotions

immobilize you.

View them as choices.

Each place along the way
is somewhere you had to be
in order to be here.

Don't be impatient

with the universe.

In God's eyes,
no one on this planet
is any better than you.

Realize that the journey
and the goal are always
the same.

Detachment is the absence of a need
to hold on to anyone or anything.
It's a way of thinking and being
that gives us the freedom to flow
with life. Detachment is the only
vehicle available to take you
from striving to arriving.

Do what you want,
as long as you're not interfering
with anyone else's right
to do the same—this is the
definition of *morality*.

So many people are *expecting*

a miracle instead of *being*

a miracle.

Being bored is a choice.
There's no such thing
as boredom in the world.

Death is nothing to fear.

It is only another dimension.

If one of us succeeds, we all do.

I send my tennis opponent
love. It removes the negativity
from my game.

You'll be trapped
emotionally and physically
until you learn to forgive.

I fill myself with love,

and I send that out into the world.

How others treat me is their path;

how I react is mine.

It's a simple procedure
to calculate the number of
seeds in an apple. But who
among us can ever say
how many apples are in a seed?

Injustice is a constant,

but you can refuse

to be seduced

into being emotionally

immobilized by it.

In the world of pure thought,
there are no boundaries;
hence, there are no limits.

I recommend being gentle

with yourself and loving yourself

unconditionally, regardless of what

comes your way.

I finally realized that other people

are simply going to be exactly

the way they are,

independent of my opinion

about them.

How could we have ever
owned anything at all?
The best that we can do
is to have temporary
possession of our toys
for a tiny speck of time.

I have a suit in my closet with the pocket cut out. It's a reminder to me that I won't be taking anything with me. The last suit I wear won't need any pockets.

You are the sum total
of all your choices
up until this moment.

Everything in the universe
is connected through thought.

Enlightenment is your

ego's greatest disappointment.

You can't always control
what goes on outside,
but you can always control
what goes on inside.

Give for the sake of giving,

and keep it circulating

as it flows back.

Fill yourself with love for everyone.

See the unfolding of God in everyone

you meet, including those whom

you've been taught to reject.

Fighting weakens,
while harmony strengthens
and empowers.

Harmony gets inside you
through your thinking.
The ancestor to all action
is a thought.

Everything you're against can be restated in a way that puts you in support of something. Instead of being against war, be for peace. Instead of being against poverty, be for prosperity. Instead of joining a war on drugs, be for purity in our youth.

Every human-made action
starts with a thought, an idea,
a vision, a mental image.
From there it materializes
into form.

If the world were so organized that everything had to be fair, no living creature could survive for a day. The birds would be forbidden to eat worms, and everyone's self-interest would have to be served.

It is love and cooperation

that makes it all work.

In the world of form,
blame is a convenient excuse
for why our world is not
exactly what we'd like it
to be. The state of the world
is a reflection of our
state of mind.

In the East, they contemplate

the forest; in the West,

they count the trees.

In the context of eternity,
time doesn't matter.

There's nothing to worry about—ever!

Either you have control or you don't.

If you do, take control; if you don't,

dismiss it. Don't waste your energy

on worry.

There's no way to happiness.
Happiness is the way.
There's no way to prosperity.
Prosperity is the way.

It's more important for you
to *be* than to have a goal.

Be in this moment.

There has always only been *NOW*.

The process of surrendering,
focusing, and living on
purpose leads to ecstasy.

It's easy to love some people.

The true test is to love someone

who's hard to love.

Send all your enemies love.

When a problem arises,
go within. Get very quiet
about it. Use it
to learn something.

Being intelligent is not being studious.

It's knowing how to be fulfilled

in all circumstances.

Yesterday is just as over
as the Peloponnesian War.

You're creating it all.

Nobody else is doing it to you.

Go beyond the ideas of succeeding

and failing—these are the judgments.

Stay in the process and allow

the universe to handle the details.

When you squeeze an orange, you get orange juice because that's what's inside. The very same principle is true about you. When someone squeezes you—puts pressure on you—what comes out is what's inside. And if you don't like what's inside, you can change it by changing your thoughts.

Stop focusing on what
you don't have, and shift
your consciousness to an
appreciation for all you are and
all that you *do* have.

Your body is nothing more than

the garage where you temporarily

park your soul.

Stop looking for
your purpose. *Be* it!

Tell me what you're for,

and I'll show you what's going

to expand in a positive way.

Tell me what you're against,

and I'll show you what's going

to expand in a destructive way.

The essence of greatness

is the ability to choose personal

fulfillment in circumstances

where others choose madness.

The fear of not *having* enough
prevents many from seeing
that they already *are* enough.

You're totally free
when you're able to stop
thinking about yourself
and your self-importance.

The more you give away,

the more you get back.

The only boundaries we have are in form. There are no obstacles in thought.

The only response to hatred is love.

Everything else will bring you down.

You can sit forever, lamenting how bad you've been, feeling guilty until your death, and not one tiny slice of that guilt will do anything to rectify past behavior.

You're the result of all the previous

pictures you've painted for yourself . . .

and you can always paint new ones.

All you get is today,
and next week maybe.
But today, for sure.

You can't get ahold of the wind.

It's the same with thought.

You can't age thought.
You can only age form.

Attachment to being right

creates suffering. When you have

a choice to be right or to be kind,

choose kindness, and watch

your suffering disappear.

Anything that immobilizes
you, gets in your way,
or keeps you from your goals is
all yours. You can throw
it away anytime you choose.

What you must do to move yourself

into the mental framework for

"miracle making" is to just let go.

Once you believe in yourself and

see your soul as divine and precious,

you'll automatically be converted

to a being who can create a miracle.

Authentic empowerment is the knowing that you are on purpose, doing God's work, peacefully and harmoniously.

Are you part of the problem

or part of the solution?

One cannot choose
up sides on a round planet.

117

Authentic empowerment is surrendering to that which is loving, harmonious, and good in ourselves, and not allowing for enemies in our consciousness.

Jesus told us that even
the least among us could
do all that he had done,
and even greater things.
You can be a miracle worker.

If you doubt the principles of the universe, they won't work for you.

To not forgive is to not understand

how the universe works

and how you fit into it.

Giving is in alignment
with your purpose.

You can't own anything

while you're here. You can't acquire

anything. Your life can only

be given away.

Love empowers you
to higher levels.

What you think about expands.

If your thoughts are centered on

what's missing, then what's missing,

by definition, will have to expand.

Nothing you imagine

in your mind is impossible.

What goes around
comes around.

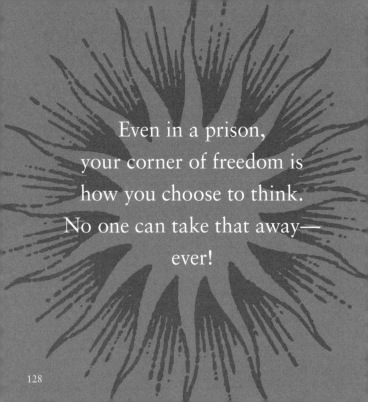

Even in a prison,
your corner of freedom is
how you choose to think.
No one can take that away—
ever!

Meditation shatters the illusion

of your separateness.

Meditation gives you an
opportunity to come to know
your invisible self.

Your lifetime in form is to be honored

and celebrated. Go beyond your

enslavement, and live fully in the now,

as this is the only time you have.

Once you've learned how to enter your inner kingdom, you have a special retreat within that's always available to you.

Everything exists for some reason

as a part of the perfect intelligence

that is the universe.

More is less;
less is more.

You're here for a reason,

and it's not to hoard

a lot of physical stuff.

Rather than put a label on yourself as

Christian, Jew, Muslim, Buddhist, or

whatever, instead make a commitment

to be Christ-like, God-like,

Buddha-like, and Mohammed-like.

There's no stress in the world,
only people thinking
stressful thoughts.

No one can create anger or stress

within you; only you can do that by

virtue of how you process your world.

How can one invisible thought
be more or less valuable than
another invisible thought?

Your inner and outer design

is perfectly in balance

with all things in the universe.

The universe provides
abundantly when you're
in a state of gratefulness.

When you know and feel the miracle

that you are, you become certain

that nothing is impossible for you.

You can never fail.
You just produce results.

Willingness to forgive
yourself is the necessary step
to being in harmony with
all the universal principles.

When it comes to addictions,

when you're pursuing poisons,

you can never get enough of what

you don't want. You become

what you think about all day long,

and those days eventually

become your lifetime.

If you meet someone

whose soul is not aligned with yours,

send them love and move along.

If you're going to follow
your bliss and make a
difference in the world,
you'll soon learn that you
can't follow the herd.

All the great teachers have left us with

a similar message: Go within,

discover your invisible higher self,

and know God as the love

that is within you.

It's in every one of us
to be love, if we allow it.

A new attitude can convert
a stifling job situation
into one of joy.

One song! That is our *uni* (one) *verse* (song). No matter how we separate into individual notes, we're all still involved in the one song.

When you judge others,
you don't define them,
you define yourself.

Our suffering is caused by the mind—

by a mind that insists on having

preferences and won't allow others

to be just as they are.

You're not stuck
where you are unless
you decide to be.

If you wonder about the difference

between attachment and enjoyment,

ask yourself how you'd react if

suddenly an object you valued

was gone.

Those who think that the
world is a dark place
are blind to the light that
might illuminate their lives.

For every act of unkindness,

there are a million kind acts.

Always remember that each day

as you look at your world and see

millions upon millions of flowers

opening up, God does it all

without using any force.

If an event happens,
it cannot unhappen in
your physical world.

You can't get prune juice from an

orange, no matter how hard you

squeeze it. You can't give hate if

you only have love inside.

You'll be happy to know that the universal law that created miracles hasn't been repealed.

When you call yourself a jerk, that's

your invisible critic judging your

outer self. Remember, what you

think about expands.

You come into this world in a wrinkled little body, and you leave in a large wrinkled body . . . if you're lucky.

There is one grand lie—
that we are limited.
The only limits we have
are the limits we believe.

Since your mind is your own private

territory, you can give any new idea

a private audition for a few days

before sharing it with others.

A mind at peace, a mind focused on not harming others, is stronger than any physical force in the universe.

Of all the deathbed regrets

that I've heard, not one of them

has been, "I wish I'd spent more

time at the office."

Be patient and loving with every

fearful thought. Practice observing

your fears as a witness

and you'll see them dissolve.

When you trust in yourself,
you trust in the wisdom
that created you.

Our lives are what

our thoughts create.

All your doubts are
obstacles inhibiting
your entry into the kingdom
of real magic.

Let go of the notion
that things shouldn't be that way.
They *are* that way!

Nothing is owned, and the sooner

you realize this, the more you'll

be able to tune in to the wondrous

principle of abundance.

Entering the magic garden
of miracles means that the
emphasis is on developing
a consciousness of possibility.

Rulers can remove our outer places of

worship, but the inner place,

that invisible corner of freedom

that is ever present in each of us,

can never be legislated.

Rather than being
against evil, be only *for* love.

The choice is up to you:

It can either be "Good morning,

God!" or "Good God, morning."

Our beliefs are the invisible
ingredients in all our activities.

Risks are nothing more than thoughts

that you've convinced yourself

are impossible to implement.

In order to forgive,
you must have blamed.

When you see yourself as connected

rather than separate,

you automatically begin to cooperate.

This is what the healing process

is all about.

As you begin to heal
the inner you, you alter
your immune system.

You create your thoughts,

your thoughts create your intentions,

and your intentions create

your reality.

To know the secret of prosperity,

know that you can never find it

outside yourself.

You are never going
to get it all;
you are it all already.

You see

what you believe,

rather than believe

what you see.

If it works any place,
it works every place.

Give up the "want." Know in your

heart that you don't need

one more thing to make yourself

complete, and then watch all those

external things become less and less

significant in your heart.

Intuition is
loving guidance.

Your soul . . . that inner,

quiet, empty space . . . is yours

to consult. It will always guide you

in the right direction.

When you know that you're
in charge of your intentions,
then you'll come to know
that you're in charge
of your entire world.

We put labels on people

and fight wars over them.

If we truly want harmony,

we have to get past the labels.

Your power and authenticity
as a person won't be measured
by duration, but by your
donations of love.

Death is a very embarrassing
event to the ego.

If you find yourself believing

that you must always be

the way you've always been,

you're arguing against growth.

Money—like health, love,
happiness, and all forms of
miraculous occurrences that
you want to create
for yourself—is the result
of living purposefully.
It is not a goal unto itself.

You are at once a beating heart

and a single heartbeat

in this body called humanity.

We are our form and our
formlessness. We are both
visible and invisible,
and we need to honor our
totality, not just what
we can see and touch.

When you allow God to speak

through you and smile upon

the earth through you—because

you're an unconditional giver,

a purposeful being—prosperity

will be your reward.

Neither your family
nor your culture gave you
your personality.
You created it yourself.

Surrender to a new consciousness,

a thought that whispers, "I can

do this thing in this moment.

I will receive all the help I need

as long as I stay with this intention

and go within for assistance."

You are eternal, and the invisible

essence of you can never die.

You have the ability to turn any

thought into form with the power

of your mind.

You become
what you think about.

Your thoughts

are all seeds

that you plant.

"The kingdom of heaven
is within you" is not
an empty cliché; it's a reality.

You're already complete
and whole, and nothing
external to yourself
in the physical world
can make you more complete.

To be attached to your physical

appearance is to ensure a lifetime

of suffering as you watch your form

go through the natural motions that

began the moment of your conception.

Refuse to let

an old person

move into your body.

Aging is simply
a learned way of being.

From the Prince of Peace:
"As ye think, so shall ye be."

The more you attach your value

and humanity to those things

outside yourself, the more you give

those things the power to control you.

You're not a human doing,

but rather a human being.

By concentrating on your
breathing, by meditating, and
by affirming aloud
your intentions, you can
reenergize yourself
on your life's journey.

Everything you know

about yourself corresponds

to a belief you're holding.

If you're still following a career path that you decided upon as a young person, ask yourself this question today: *Would I seek out the advice of a teenager for vocational guidance?*

Inner commitment to your own

excellence is the stuff

of which miracles are made.

Conflict cannot survive
without your participation.

Death is a concept
that refers to endings.
Endings need boundaries,
and your dimensionless self
has no boundaries.

Empowerment is the inner joy

of knowing that external force

isn't necessary to be at harmony

with oneself.

Those who injured us only did

what they knew how to do,

given the conditions of their lives.

If you won't forgive, then you allow

those ancient injuries to continue

their hold on you.

What you think and talk
about expands into action.

Look at every obstacle

as an opportunity.

Enlightenment demands
that you take responsibility
for your way of life.

Forgiveness is an act
of the heart.

Be consistently aware of the need

to serve God and others in any and all

of your actions. That is the way

of the miracle worker.

Giving and receiving

are the same.

God will work with you,
not for you.

Everything we fight
only weakens us,
and hinders our ability
to see the opportunity
in the obstacle.

The entire universe

is an intelligence system.

When you're told that you have

some kind of physical affliction,

you can either prepare to suffer

or prepare to heal.

Your will is the gardener that tends

the garden called your body.

Listen to your body

and it will tell you

what you need to know.

The principles of abundance, synchronicity, detachment, and oneness are operative in the universe. All you have to do is tune in to them and let them work through you.

A tree allows the life force to work

naturally through it.

You have the power within

your thoughts to be as natural

as the tree.

Spiritual beings

keep their thoughts focused

on love and harmony.

Live one day at a time,
emphasizing ethics
rather than rules.

Turn away from outer accumulation

and achievement, and allow yourself

to be purposeful and guided.

You, a person with a vision,
are like a pebble in a stream,
moving ever outward
to infinity, impacting all who
come into contact
with the ripple.

Intuitive feelings always guide you

in a direction of growth

and purposefulness.

Within you is the kingdom
of serenity that can create
all the prosperity
you could ever want.

Intentions are the energy
of your soul coming
into contact with
your physical reality.

Releasing judgment

of another is actually releasing

judgment of yourself.

If you can conceive it

in your mind, then it can be brought

into your physical world.

We send our kids off to school
to major in "labeling"
and think the ones who do
it best deserve
the highest grades.

Miracles come

in moments.

Be ready and willing.

The real measure
of your humanity
is in your soul.

Anything you desire
to do, you can do—*anything!*

Your mind is unbound,

formless, and infinitely capable

of choosing any kind of miracle

it desires, when it's

fully honored and celebrated.

Just as each flower has its own
unique color—even though it
originates from only one light—
each individual, although unique
in appearance, comes from one
essence as well.

Live forgiveness
every day rather than just
talking about it on Sunday.

Ask for nothing
and you will receive much.

You are alone and all one—

all at the same time.

The more you try
to force something
for your own benefit,
the less you'll enjoy
what you're seeking
so desperately.

Everything is already here

in the world. Where else

would it be?

Your purpose is always
about giving, loving, and
serving in some capacity.

You are a soul with a body

rather than a body with a soul.

Allow yourself the luxury

of believing in the divinity

of your own soul.

Your very essence
is an invisible intelligence.
Your essence is in thought,
where it's virtually impossible
to have attachment.

Who you are is located
in the dimensionless realm
that we call your thoughts.

Creating money is just like creating

anything else in your life:

It involves not being attached to it,

and not giving it power

over your life in any way.

Suffering is always played out in form.

It is not you who suffers, only the

person you imagine yourself to be.

All you have become
is the result of all
you have thought.

Surrendering is an act
of the heart. How do you
surrender? Just let go.

You are intelligence within your form,

just as the rose is an intelligence

that delivers the fragrance

and appearance of a flower.

Abundance flows

when we love

what we're doing.

Everything you're currently
against blocks you
from abundance.

Miracles can only happen
when you get rid of
the concept of "impossible"
and allow yourself
to experience the magic
of knowing.

The first step toward discarding

a scarcity mentality involves

giving thanks for everything

that you are and everything

that you have.

Acting as if you were already

what you want to become

and knowing that you can become it

is the way to remove self-doubt

and enter your blissful kingdom.

There must be bliss
and harmony within
in order for you to know
miracles.

Have in your mind that which

would constitute a miracle for you.

Get the vision. Suspend disbelief

and skepticism.

Examine what you believe to be impossible, and then change your beliefs.

We talk privately to God and call it prayer. So then why does a return call seem so far-fetched, particularly if we believe that there's some universal intelligence out there that we're addressing?

Enlightenment is the quiet
acceptance of what is.

When we love ourselves, we
refuse to allow others
to manage our emotions
from afar. Forgiveness
is our means to that end.

Forgiveness is the ability

to give love away in the most difficult

of circumstances.

Giving is the key
to forgiving.

Some of the most despicable human

behavior has been conducted

in the name of "I'm only following

the law" or "I'm just doing my job."

If we are to have magical bodies,

we must have magical minds.

Treasure your physical being
as a vehicle that houses
your soul. Once you have
the inner way, the outer way
will follow.

We receive only that
which we're willing to let in.

Create an inner harmony

where your loving soul guides

your physical behavior, rather than

having your soul always come in

second place.

Surrendering is trusting in the forces

and principles that are always at work

in this perfect universe.

The reality of life
speaks to us in silence.

Forgiveness is humanity's
highest achievement because it
shows true enlightenment
in action. It shows that one is
in touch with the energy
of love.

Judgment means that you view

the world as *you* are,

rather than as *it* is.

Love is giving,

and it has nothing to do with

what you receive.

Your miracles are
an inside job.
Go there to create
the magic you seek
in your life.

If you're committed to seeing

your physical self with wonder

and awe, and if you can know deep

within that your invisible self wants

the body it inhabits to be as healthy

as possible, then you're a student

who is ready.

Your limits are defined
by the agreement you've made
about what's possible.
Change that agreement
and you can dissolve all limits.

This total being called
"human being" can't function
harmoniously when the
components are in conflict.

The way to oneness

seems to be through the path

of inner harmony.

The way to inner harmony is

through silence.

The dying process

in the physical world

allows you to live.

There are no accidents
in a perfect universe.

We're all part
of infinity.

A few minutes spent in total awe

will contribute to your spiritual

awakening faster than

any metaphysics course.

We all come from *no where* to *now here* to *no where*. It's all the same. It's all one.

Purpose is about giving yourself

unconditionally and accepting what

comes back with love,

even if what comes back

isn't what you'd anticipated.

Being a spiritual being
involves being able to touch
your invisible self.

In the dimensionless world

of thought, everything is possible.

Go within to the peaceful solitude

of your mind. It is there that you'll

discover God.

It is all perfect,
this universe we're in.
Slow down and enjoy it all.

About the Author

Wayne W. Dyer, Ph.D., is an internationally renowned author and speaker in the field of self-development. He's the author of more than 20 books; has created many audios, CDs, and videos; and has appeared on thousands of television and radio programs. Five of his books, *Manifest Your Destiny, Wisdom of the Ages, There's a Spiritual Solution to Every Problem,* and the *New York Times* bestsellers *10 Secrets for Success and Inner Peace* and *The Power of Intention* were featured as National Public Television specials.

Dyer holds a doctorate in educational counseling from Wayne State University and was an associate professor at St. John's University in New York.

Website: **www.DrWayneDyer.com**

Hay House Lifestyles
Titles of Related Interest

Empowerment Cards (a 50-card deck), by Tavis Smiley

Everyday Positive Thinking, by Louise L. Hay

Feng Shui Dos & Taboos for Health and Well-being,
by Angi Ma Wong

Meditations, by Sylvia Browne

The Power of Intention Cards (a 50-card deck),
by Dr. Wayne W. Dyer

Simple Things, by Jim Brickman, with Cindy Pearlman

Wisdom of the Heart, by Alan Cohen

All of the above are available at your local bookstore,
or may be ordered by visiting:
Hay House USA: **www.hayhouse.com**
Hay House Australia: **www.hayhouse.com.au**
Hay House UK: **www.hayhouse.co.uk**
Hay House South Africa: **orders@psdprom.co.za**

Notes

Notes

Notes

Notes

We hope you enjoyed this Hay House Lifestyles book.
If you would like to receive a free catalog featuring additional
Hay House books and products, or if you would like information
about the Hay Foundation, please contact:

Hay House, Inc.
P.O. Box 5100
Carlsbad, CA 92018-5100

(760) 431-7695 or (800) 654-5126
(760) 431-6948 (fax) or (800) 650-5115 (fax)
www.hayhouse.com

Published and distributed in Australia by: Hay House Australia Pty. Ltd.
18/36 Ralph St. • Alexandria NSW 2015 • *Phone:* 612-9669-4299
Fax: 612-9669-4144 • www.hayhouse.com.au

Published and distributed in the United Kingdom by:
Hay House UK, Ltd. • Unit 62, Canalot Studios
222 Kensal Rd., London W10 5BN • *Phone:* 44-20-8962-1230
Fax: 44-20-8962-1239 • www.hayhouse.co.uk

Published and distributed in the Republic of South Africa by:
Hay House SA (Pty), Ltd., P.O. Box 990, Witkoppen 2068
Phone/Fax: 2711-7012233 • orders@psdprom.co.za

Distributed in Canada by: Raincoast
9050 Shaughnessy St., Vancouver, B.C. V6P 6E5
Phone: (604) 323-7100 • *Fax:* (604) 323-2600

Sign up via the Hay House USA Website to receive the Hay House online newsletter and stay informed about what's going on with your favorite authors. You'll receive bimonthly announcements about: Discounts and Offers, Special Events, Product Highlights, Free Excerpts, Giveaways, and more!
www.hayhouse.com